Workbook Eight
Of the Business Essentials
Series

CHAMPION TEAM WITH A
CHAMPION LEADER

John Millar

ISBN:1537341545
ISBN-13:9781537341545

DEDICATION

I dedicate this book to my mother and father, who raised me while self-employed. They taught me to work hard and listen to everyone but to make my own choices as to what is right and what is wrong.. and oh, did I mention work hard?

Anyone who tells you to work smart not hard hasn't ever done it tough and realized that if you work smart AND hard you will achieve more than you can possibly dream.

CONTENTS

PRODUCT DESCRIPTION

Developing a loyal championship team that is willing to stand in the heat for you, win for you, follow you and rejoice with you, is the result of directed, well-placed and guided intention and training. It doesn't just happen. In fact, look at a disjointed group of selfish employees that lazily hang about a workplace trying to get away with producing as little as possible and I'll show you a team that lacks direction and leadership.

This DVD is all about developing that champion team that will deliver; that will withstand difficulties for the sake of the business and for you. It's no joke that your team is only as strong as its weakest link. Have a look at the ones on your team who are under-performing. This is how strong you are – or aren't.

In this DVD we will look at the 5 traits of a champion leader and evaluate the best ways in which you can adopt them so they become a daily part of your routines. We evaluate the best ways in which to apply these characteristics to your business and how to reap the results.

The 5 Traits of a CHAMPION Leader

These five characteristics of a CHAMPION can be applied within businesses in two ways:

As a standard against which leaders must be measured and

As a standard against which all potential team members are measured and held accountable.

1. Commitment
Leaders need to know how to gain commitment to a compelling vision and the strategies that are used to achieve it. This also includes investing the time and energy in creating that compelling vision and strategies and having the courage to ask for help in achieving it. This comes from leaders who know how to communicate in a way that influences their team members in a positive way. It's a way of communicating that shows how each individual team member benefits when the organization fulfills its vision and strategy, gaining buy-in from all.

2. Humility
Leaders must lead by example in setting the expectation of constant and never ending improvement, and they show it by being open to feedback from all sources. This means more than just proclaiming there is an "open door" policy. It must be demonstrated by actually taking feedback and accepting appreciation for that feedback by saying 'thank you.' There is no need for justification, explanation, recriminations or blame. Accepting comment and suggestion from everyone is one of the greatest ways to display your humility and concern for all.

3. Accountability
Being accountable for decisions, outcomes, results, mistakes and errors is all part of creating a work-place environment in which all members are valued and cared for. It engenders maturity, innovation, stake-holder thinking and team support. And it all begins with you. It doesn't have to be scary – in fact it can be invigorating

and exciting. It's not about creating a blame-game – on the contrary it's all about creating a mature, well-developed, evolutionary work place where everyone gets to be part of the decision process.

4. Motivation

Motivation is more than just "hard work" and "long hours." It means being inspired to take action, even with difficult decisions and challenging situations. It means avoiding procrastination at all costs and refusing to tolerate things that do not improve the organization. And it means supporting the best efforts of team members.

Leaders must understand human motivation and apply the following assumptions in their approach:

Everyone on the team wants to do a good job

Actions/decisions are always done with positive intent with the best resources individuals have available to them at the time

People want to be recognized for their contributions

People are motivated by intrinsic factors

5. Preparation

Leaders must also lead by example and set the tone for their organization. This preparation and organisation is vital to your ongoing business success. It means that leaders should be certain any meetings they hold are designed in a way in which all those invited are aware of their role and the purpose for their inclusion. Agendas and meeting outcomes should be clearly communicated. Schedules should be well maintained and projected as far in to the future as possible while offering enough flexibility to allow for reasonable adjustments.

The leader should be continually looking for ways to raise the bar on individual and organizational preparation. This includes punctuality, meeting deadlines, returning phone calls, and planning the year, quarter, month, weeks and days to maximize results.

- This is about having the right people on the bus. It starts with you however so you'll learn how to maximise your own skills and then you will attract and retain the right people.

- When you understand how the TEAM is the most important part of your business and what needs to be done to achieve the very best from yourself and others, you are well on your way to becoming a better manager of this invaluable resource.

Regards,

John Millar

> There are usually three common frustrations common in most businesses which are time, the team and the money.

They're all interlinked and a lot of it flows in and around the team. So, with a good quality team, you can achieve so much more.

How can you get your team to work for you, your business, your customers and themselves?

1. _____

2. _____

3. _____

4 _____

5. _____

> They're all interlinked and a lot of it flows in and around the team. So, with a good quality team, you can achieve so much more.

When we're looking at the business remember there's a specific cycle within a business where you look after the team, the team looks after the customer and the customer looks after the business and business then in turn looks after you as the business owner.

_____

_____

_____

_____

_____

_____

_____

Team actually is an acronym that stands for

Together
Everyone
Achieves
More

....

....

....

....

....

....

> **We must actually be able to work in complete synergy and harmony together and that's what makes a team.**

- Everyone stand in a circle
- Throw the ball to someone else in the circle.
- Call their name every time you throw to them. This person is YOUR catcher until instructed otherwise.
- Whoever throws the ball first will become the last catcher.
- Add extra balls and see if you can keep them all in the air, once you have this working reverse the direction.

....

....

....

....

....

What did you learn from the game?

Write the top 3 things you learnt from the game

1. ....

2. ....

3. ....

How does this relate to you and your business?

1. ....

2. ....

3. ....

4. ....

5. ....

Remember games are often a reflection of behavior. You'll actually start to see some of the things and some of the attitudes that people use within a game that they actually have in their real life and within their working environment. So, if some people become petulant and walk off, other people will become frustrated, other people will become more joyful and engaged, other people will start bossing other people around, some people will want to wait getting instruction.

Make sure you recap the activity, making note of those things for all of your participants and then sit down and look at what are the top three things that you've learned and encourage your team to come back to you with the top three things that they learned from within that game.

In the top left hand, at bottom left hand quadrant where people have a low respect for themselves and a low respect for others, they usually act in a very manipulative, aggressive way and their whole attitude of working style is in lose, lose situation.

In the top left hand quadrant, we then look at somebody who's got a high level of self-respect but has a low level of respect for others. They're usually people who act in a very hostile and aggressive manner towards others. They can become very defensive and they work very much along the lines of a win-lose. They win, but everybody else loses.

In the bottom right hand quadrant, you can see there that they have a high respect for others, but low respect for themselves and that will then create rather very passive individuals. And quite often, nice people will actually evince the attitude of a lose-win situation. So, they're quite happy to make a loss to help other people win.

If we look in the top right hand quadrant, we can see that we see people with a high self-respect and a high respect for others. And they're people who can be quite assertive, but still working very much a win-win situation. In other words, I win-win, you win.

When you win, I win. It sounds the same, but really it's that win-win situation we're looking for.

HIGH

SELF PERFECT

I AM OK		I AM OK
YOU ARE NOT OK		YOU ARE OK
I AM NOT OK		I AM NOT OK
YOU ARE NOT OK		YOU ARE OK

LOW   *HIGH*

So, if we look at it again, we look at somebody who has a living style where they've got low self-respect and low respect for others, they're going to be living by the attitude of: well, I'm not okay and you're not okay. In the top left hand quadrant where they've got high self-respect, but low respect for others, their attitude is:

I'm okay, but you're not okay. Bottom right hand side, high respect for others, low respect for themselves:
I'm not okay, but it's okay because you're okay.

And then the top right hand side, some of your people with high self-esteem, which is what we want to develop as managers and business owners and a high respect for others, their whole attitude revolves around: I'm okay and you're okay. And this then creates a whole culture within an organization. This then
helps this whole attitude of being able to move things forward.

> These things all add up to our quality of life

How can you be a better leader?

1. ....
2. ....
3. ....
4. ....
5. ....
6. ....
7. ....
8. ....
9. ....
10. ....

Let's have look at the individual keys to a winning team

First and foremost, it's your right and obligation as a business owner to make sure that you provide strong leadership.

A good quality leader will show strong passion for their business and what their business stands for.

As a leader, we must take full responsibility and accountability for what actually happens.

Can we take responsibility and accountability for those things which are not our fault?

Do we deal with the body, the mind, the heart and the spirit of our team?

Are they healthy, happy, well-educated and highly trained people?

We want to take perturbation stress or those changes which are negative out and make sure that it has a positive outcomes in our lives and inside our business.

The theory of perturbation is a really great one

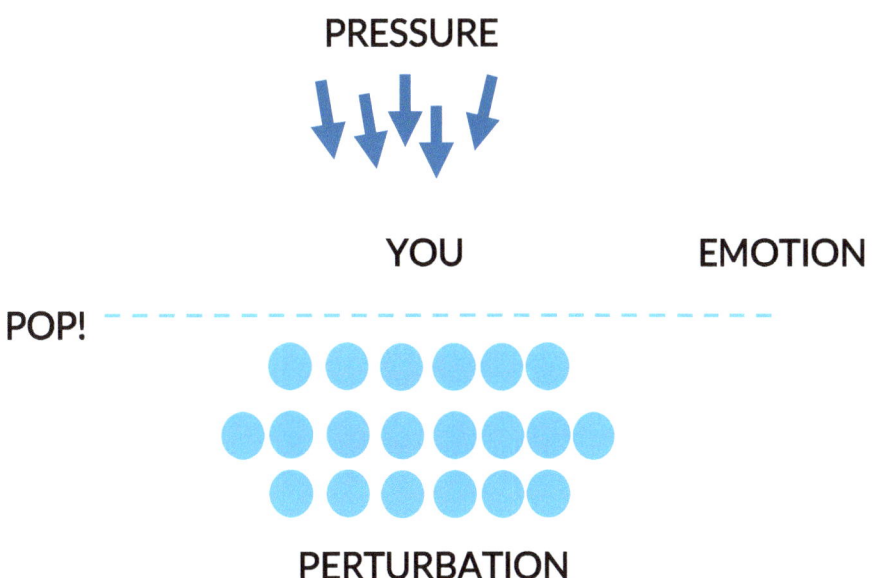

We grow the most when we move beyond our boundaries of where we're comfortable.

When we actually create those breakthroughs, it's actually going to create a bit of a breakdown. It will break apart a lot of the norms and attitudes that you've been carrying and perhaps some of the head trash that you've been working around with. You'll actually break with a lot of traditions and ideologies that have been holding you back. And once you've actually done that, you can break up what were you going to move forward in the manageable bite size chance that you can then use within your business.

Our business and our lives is so inextricably linked and our quality of life really comes down to a number of different areas.

Quality of Life

Quality of Results

Quality of Actions

Quality of Decisions

Quality of Questions

Quality of Beliefs/Dreams

Quality of Knowledge / Educations

Quality of Mentor / Teacher

First, it actually deals with the quality of the mentor, coach, and teacher Once you've got more better knowledge and education, you can then actually have much clearer beliefs and dreams that are based upon reality, not just fear.

Remember fear is:

False

Expectations

Appearing

Real

Once we actually have better beliefs and dreams, structures in place, we can then actually ask of ourselves and others far better qualities of questions, so that we can actually continually challenge and therefore grow in the way we're doing things.

Once we ask better questions, we can actually have a much better quality of our decisions because we're now making decisions based upon all the right reasons, not just our gut. That will then create a quality of action or outcome which will then produce a high quality of result and that quality of result then deals with the quality of life that we're able to have as business owners.

....

....

....

....

....

Write down the top 5 things that you can do straight away to become a better leader.

1. ....

2. ....

3. ....

4. ....

5. ....

What are the 5 areas that you perhaps either not doing well or doing that you shouldn't be doing or not doing that you should to be able to improve your leadership skills?

1. ....

2. ....

3. ....

4. ....

5. ....

How are you going to do it?

What sort of resources that you're going to need?

What training or assistance will you need to get there?

It's usually small things done consistently, that can have the largest outcome and result

....

....

....

....

....

Sit down with your mentor, consultant, coach, business partner and talk to them about those things.

The next most important key to a winning team.

Without that common goal, you are working in completely different directions to where your team might be and they might not necessarily understand things.

....

....

....

....

....

....

....

....

....

....

> **As good leaders, we must create a clear vision that enrolls and inspires.**

What do we mean by enroll and inspire?

We want people who are actively engaged in your business.

> If you can get your team to 80% of your inspiration and aspirational attitudes then you're on the way there.

....
....
....
....
....
....

It's actually going to show them what we're going to do, how we're going to do it, what sign post we're going to pass and how we're going to actually determine where we're actually at within our business.

In setting that mission, we actually have to set some really good strong goals You must have direction and focus and that direction and focus must be absolutely clear.

Goals really must be smart goals and smart remember stands for

Specific,
Measurable,
Achievable
Result Focused
Time Frame Driven

....
....
....

The third point within the keys to a winning team is all about the rules of the game.

1. Be willing to support our purpose, games, rules and goals.

2. Speak supportively.

3.Acknowledge whatever is being communicated as true for the speaker at that moment.

4. Complete your agreements. (Responsibility).

(a) Make only agreements that you are willing and intend to keep.

(b) Communicate any potential broken agreement at the first appropriate time.

(c) Clear up any broken agreement at the first appropriate opportunity.

5. If a problem arises, communicate it at the first appropriate opportunity to the person who can do something about it.

6. Be effective and efficient. (Optimize every moment....

7. Have the willingness to win and allow others to win. (Win/Win)

8. Focus on what works.

9. Agree to agree.

10. Always make sure that your role in the business is covered.

11. Have your job completely handled by the deadline set forth in your job description and list of duties.

12. Write all requests or suggestions down on an Action Request Card, including time and date that it is written, for our team meetings. Be sure to write down what time you will need whatever it is you are requesting. All Action Requests go to the Team "IN" box. Remember to follow up your requests and suggestions before the end of the

13. Acknowledge whatever did not work as well as it could have in the business and write down all suggestions for improvement. Be responsible for writing down these things so we can update our systems and improve our business together.

14. Be responsible for being clear on your duties and responsibilities.

15. Keep all time agreements.

16. Wear clothing and or uniforms (as appropriate) that is clean, pressed, and in good taste.

17. Leave other team members undisturbed. Do not add to or take away from their experience and focus at the workplace.

18. Maintain a professional demeanor at all times.

19. Handle any upsets away from the hearing of any other team members or clients.

20. Attend all team meetings scheduled; unless agreed by the business owner that you miss a meeting. Partner with another team member. If your "partner" is out of the room, be responsible to get information to them for missed meetings.

21. At all times report and communicate to your direct report and team members your whereabouts so that at all times you can be contacted for any job that may be needed to be done.

22. All team members should be at the workplace at least 10 minutes before work begins so that you can be prepared to focus on your day on or before your scheduled start time.

23. Keep your work area and the business in general clean and safe at all times.

24. Have fun and help others to do so.

What are the rules of the game for your business?

1. ....
2. ....
3. ....
4. ....
5. ....
6. ....
7. ....
8. ....
9. ....
10. ....
11. ....
12. ....
13. ....
14. ....
15. ....
16. ....
17. ....
18. ....
19. ....
20. ....

Are your customers part of your team?

Are your suppliers part of your team?

Does everybody in your business have clear rules of the game and what they're actually doing to adhere to them?

....

....

....

LOOSE : TIGHT CULTURE

TIGHT - RULES - CULTURE - CONTEXT

LOOSE - PEOPLE - CONTENT

We want set up our business so that we're creating the culture of a small business, but we're systemizing and creating a process like a corporate.

....

....

....

....

....

Once you got those rules of the game clear, you've got to have a clear action plan.

Who is going to do what?

What do they actually do?

Who does what by when?

What resources do you need?

What are the tools?

Are there specific training?

Does it interrelate with other areas of goals and actions that you're actually undertaking or is one thing actually separate?

....

....

....

If you don't clearly document and create manuals on every aspect of your business, unfortunately, you're going to have to continue to do those same things, time and time and time

Make sure that your action plan includes your business plan.

Look at supporting risk taking within a business.

Now, am I talking about occupational health and safety risks? No, I'm talking about giving people the opportunity to step up. Let them make mistakes because like you, others learn more from when they've had the opportunity to make those mistakes.

If you don't support risk taking then you don't support growth and create real opportunity within your business.

The whole concept behind kaizen is constant and never ending improvement

You can't plant a tree and say, look I want you stop at exactly 900 cm tall. If it's designed and its nature allows it to grow to many meters in height, it will continue to grow and develop, grow, plateau, grow, plateau and so should we and so should our team and our business.

We need to make sure that we've got 100% involvement and inclusion within our team.

You as a leader must take leadership or give other people that leadership role to drive your business forward and so that they can share their journey with us and ensure we're going together in the same direction.

Squares Game

Get into teams of no more than 5 people. Find a space on the floor and sit in a circle ...

RULES OF THIS GAME ...

1. NO Talking ... Including grunts, moans and giggles ...

2. NO Taking Pieces ... Must accept pieces ...

3. NO Gesturing ... Including eyes, nods and pointing ...

4. NO Helping ...

5. YOU CAN PASS ...

6. To WIN, you must each complete a square ...

7. This is a game about communication, the only way to communicate is to PASS

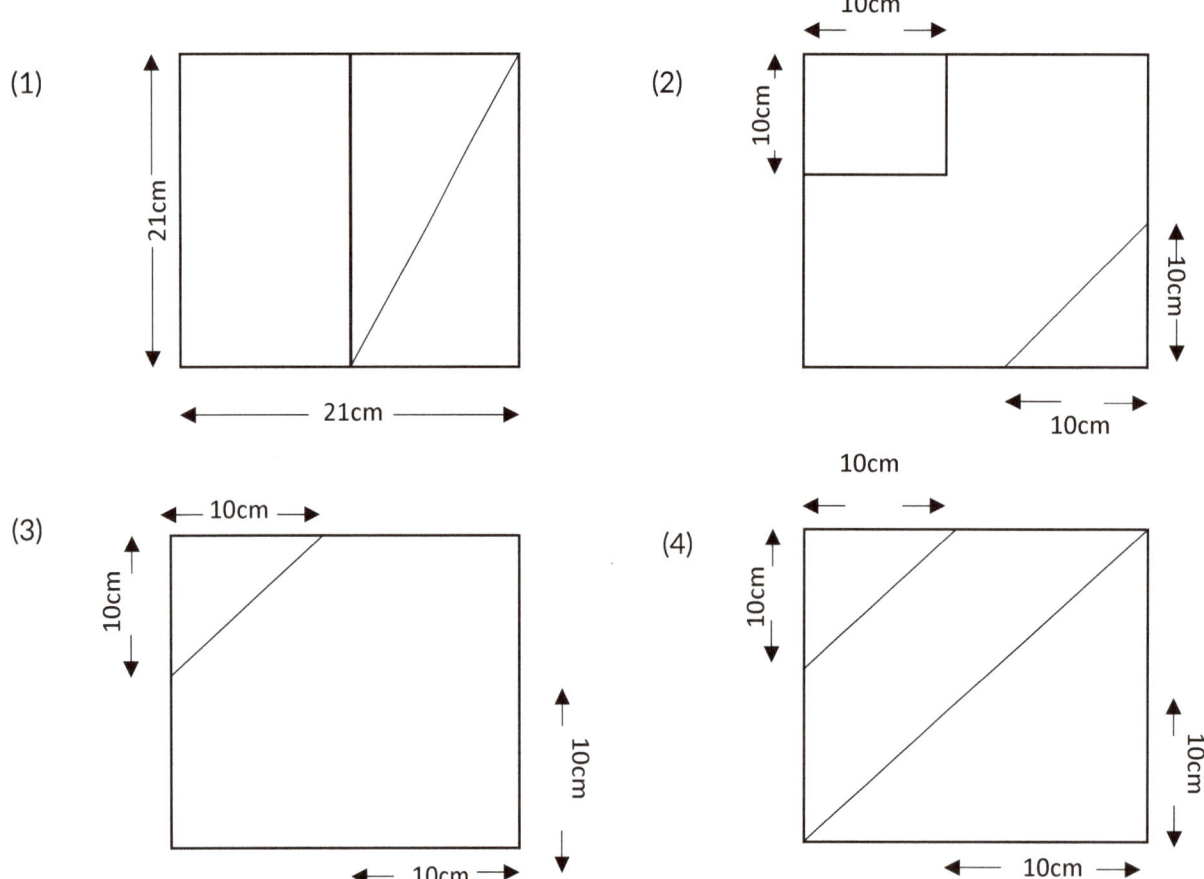

(5)

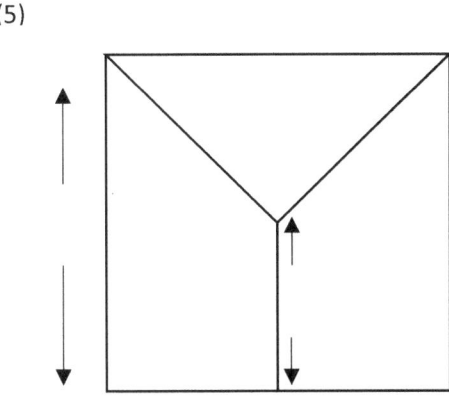

21cm

(1)

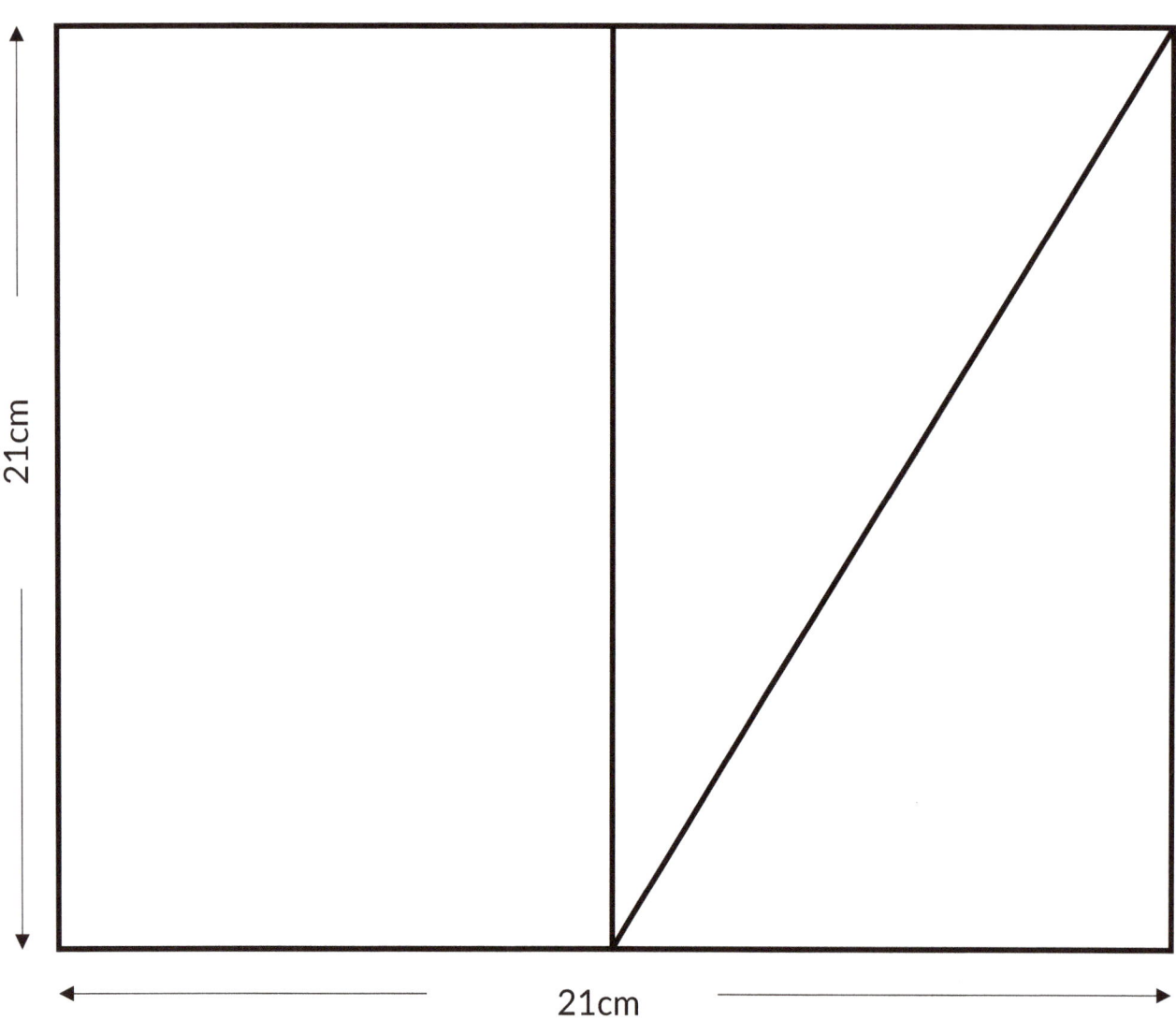

21cm

21cm

(2)

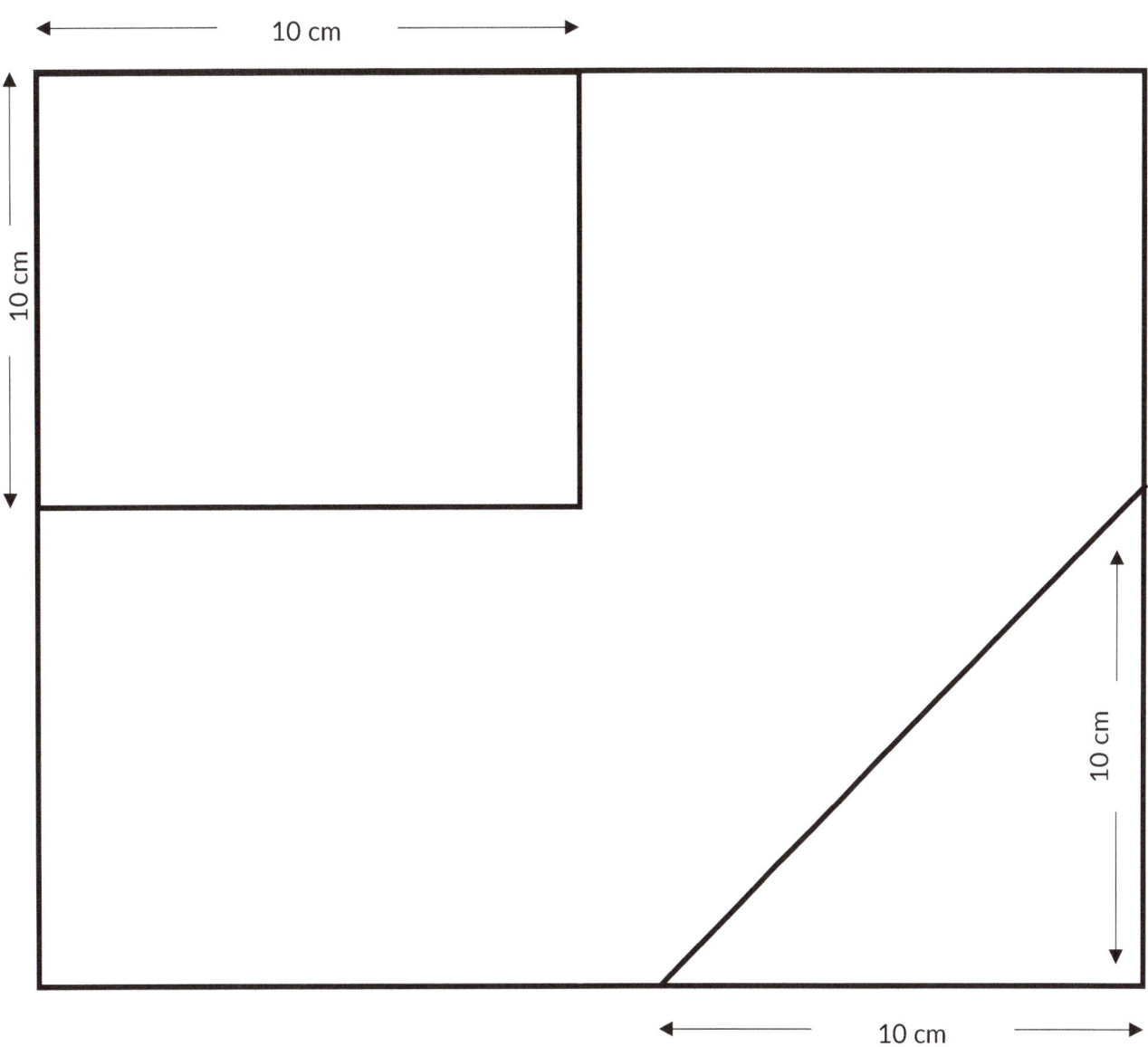

(3)

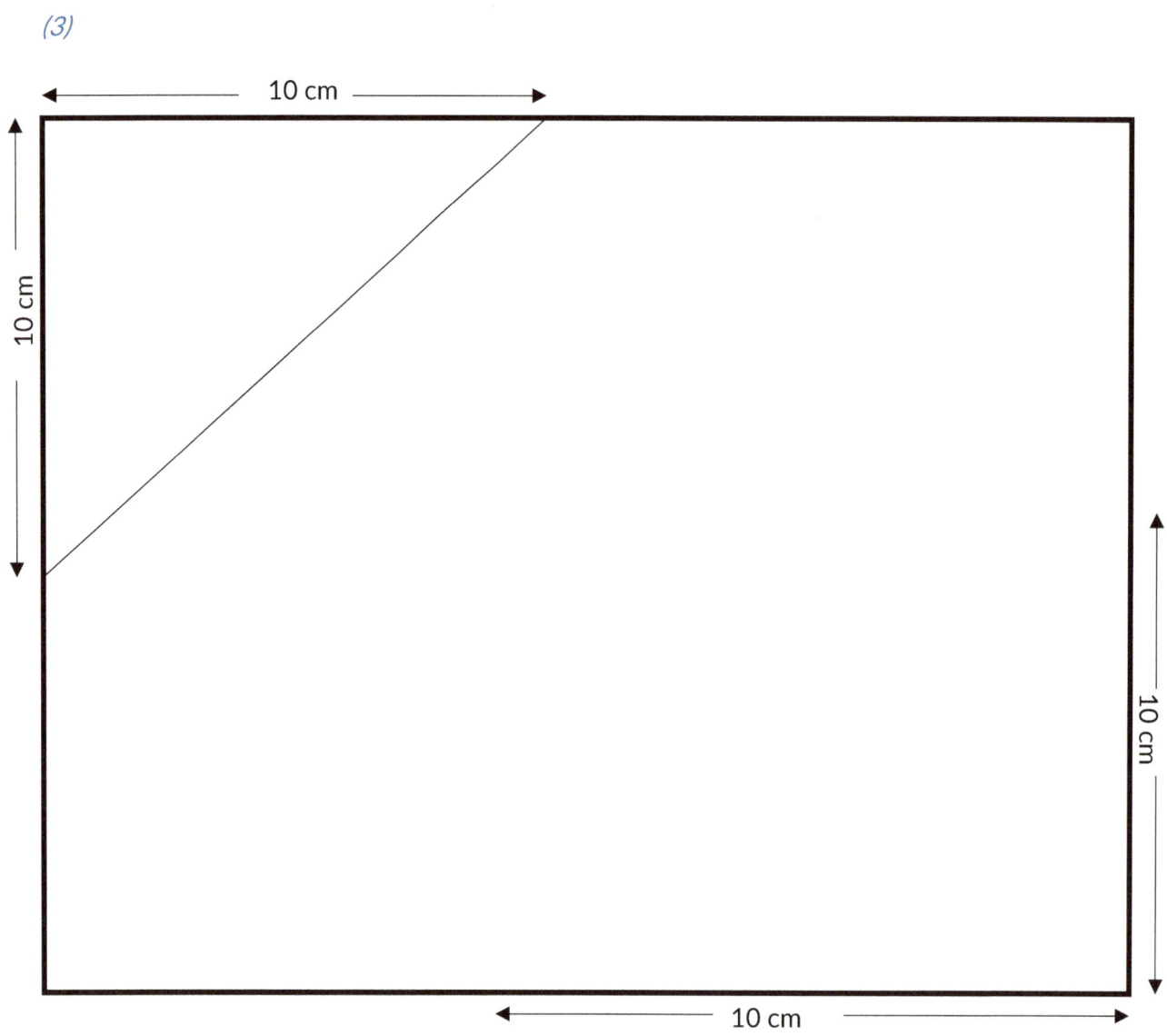

(4)

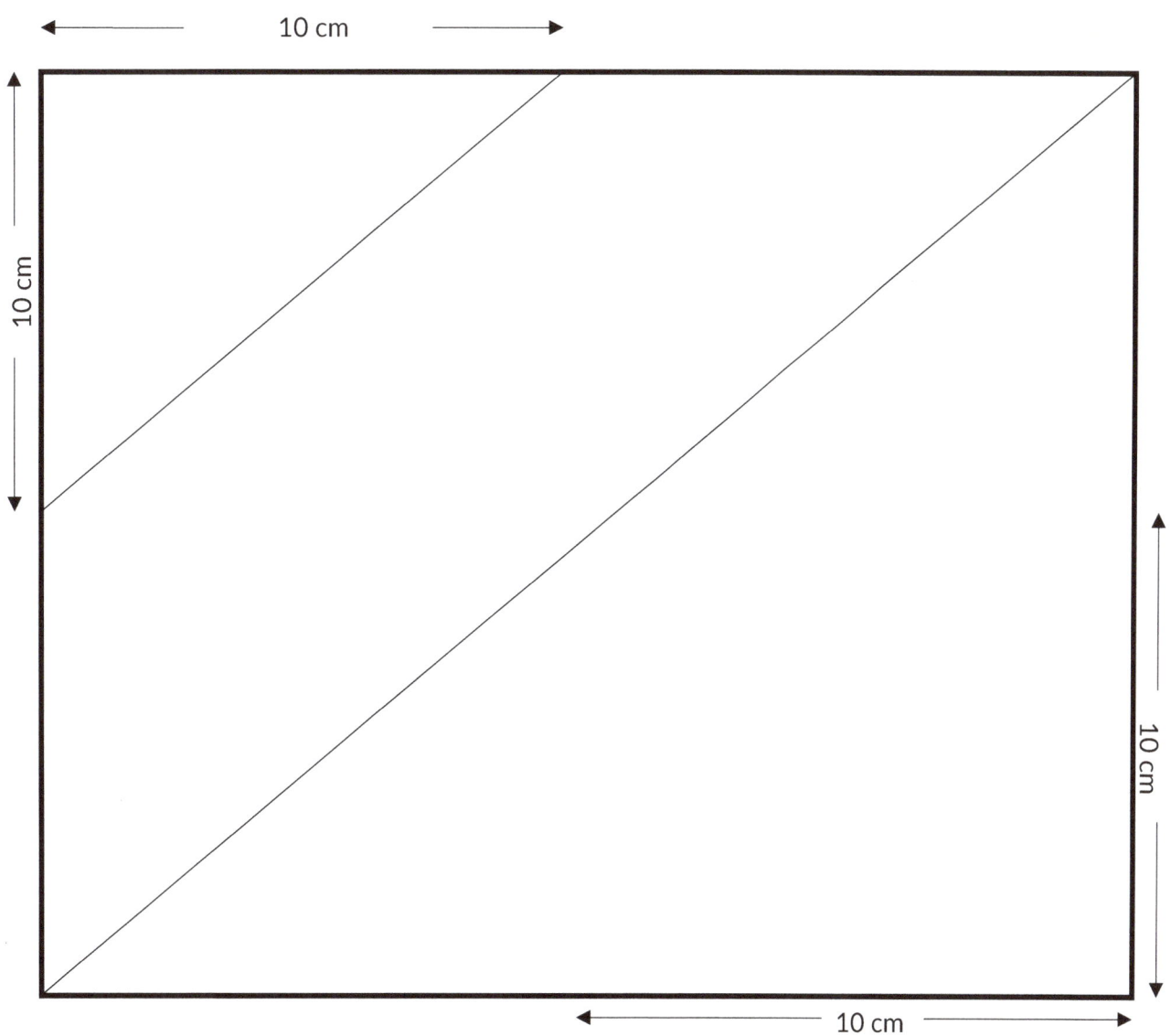

10 cm

10 cm

10 cm

10 cm

(5)

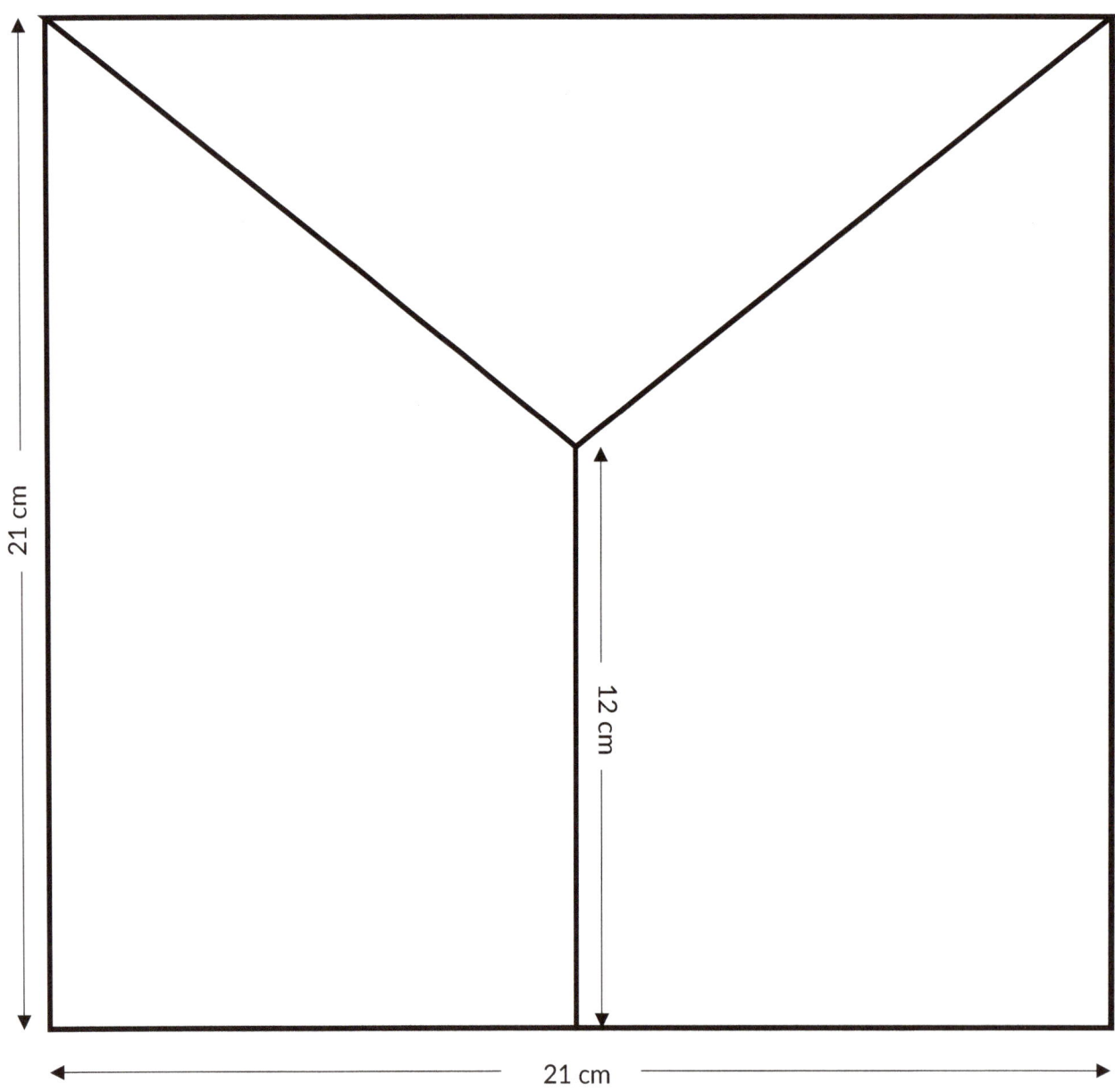

21 cm

12 cm

21 cm

> True Communication is the response that you get.

One of the really big rituals that I love introducing to any new business that I work with and my team works with is what's called the WIFLE

THE RULES OF A WIFLE SESSION:

1. A WIFLE commences with all participants seated...

2. All participants take-a turn to express themselves. All WIFLES commence with the words, "What 1 feel like saying is..."

3. There is to be NO talking, responding or comments by any other team member during another team members' WIFLE...

4. All participants finish their WIFLE with the words, "That's what 1 feel like expressing". At this time other team members will reply with, "Thanks NAME".

5. The WIFLE is passed to the next team member by turning to the person on your left and saying, "And NAME what do you feel like saying?"

6. If required the team may then have a burning issue session ... Where any issues that have come up because of other team members comments may be discussed.

7. Once everyone has had their WIFLE the session is completed with a WOOOOOSH.

> We must have correction within any organization without invalidation.
> Regular team meetings are very important within the business.

I know that if you take this information away and you apply it specifically within your business, that you will get the results that you deserve, you will get the outcomes that you need to have a truly successful business. I look forward to seeing you on one of our workshops, trainings, seminars and webinars – anything that's going to be involved with us. We love helping you and we'd love to hear your suggestions. I promise you, you will achieve the results that you deserve based on what you do or don't do with this information.

John Millar

Business Essentials Series...

Disc 1 in the Business Essentials Series
Gaining Focus in Your Business

*This is about your fundamental learning skills and what you will need to do to change them to vastly improve the way you look
at your development to become a truly effective business owner not just simply remain self-employed.*

You will also give you some excellent tools to set goals, work on your plans and create a diary that will allow you to steal your time back to begin moving your business from chaos to control.

Disc 2 in the Business Essentials Series
Getting Your Financials Right

You will learn the importance of understanding your financials.

After all being in business is about making profit and having cash flow work for YOU since you are responsible for your profits.
Become your accountant and book keepers best friend by understanding more about how the financials in your business works so you can ask them better questions to maximise your profits not simply ensure tax compliance.

Disc 3 in the Business Essentials Series
Leveraging Your Business Harder

You will learn the principles of what and how to leverage far more in your business to get more from less and to work far smarter and not just harder.

Here is where you will receive some of the tools you will need to better understand how to get your business flying, what it is you need to test and measure, how to do it and WHY it's so important.

Disc 4 in the Business Essentials Series
How to Generate More Clients Profitably

This is where you will determine your uniqueness, develop a meaningful guarantee and learn the basics of good advertising.

You will gain a better appreciation between the difference of Marketing and Advertising, learn how to get the most for the least investment and ensure that you do it all profitably.

Disc 5 in the Business Essentials Series
Maximising Your Conversion Rates

Get to know how your Sales Pipeline REALLY works and how to identify who your suspects really are, convert prospects into regular shoppers and understand how much more work you can do to maximise your sales experience.

Disc 6 in the Business Essentials Series
Meet and Exceed Your Clients Expectations

Now you have new customers, how do you make sure you KEEP them, how do you wanting to come back time and again while telling their friends? ...this is where you really make a difference.

Disc 7 in the Business Essentials Series
Systemising Your Business For Consistent Excellence

Do you recognise the importance of having systems in your business and how they can improve your profitability?

We show you how to systemise like a corporate while retaining the culture of a smaller business. Understanding how we systemise for routine and humanise for the exceptions will enable you to be the best in your field every time.

Disc 8 in the Business Essentials Series

Do You Have a Champion Team with a Champion Leader?

This is about having the right people on the bus. It starts with you however so you'll learn how to maximise your own skills and then you will attract and retain the right people.

When you understand how the TEAM is the most important part of your business and what needs to be done to achieve the very best from yourselves and others you are well on your way to becoming a better manager of this invaluable resource.

Disc 9 in the Business Essentials Series

The Essentials of Getting Your Time Back.

This is where you get to redefine your time management You will understand better how you can start working far more on the business than in the business than ever before.

You will also finally find out why others can seem to fit more into their day while having a great LIFE – WORK balance (notice the order!)..

Disc 10 in the Business Essentials Series

Simply Brilliant Customer Service.

It's so easy to give mediocre or good customer service but it's just as easy to give amazing service to your customers and delight them.

You will understand the simple easy steps that you must take to provide consistently brilliant service and how to get your team excited about doing it.

Disc 11 in the Business Essentials Series

Discovering DISC and EQ not just IQ.

We believe for things to change first you must change so here you will learn why you behave as you do and just as importantly understand why other people react and act the way they do.

You will also learn what DISC really is and what it isn't. You will learn how to apply these important principles in your recruitment and team management / development.

You will learn how to use these ideas in creating a more dynamic team and discover the what and why of emotional intelligence. You will also develop key strategies for using the knowledge here and the tools we have available on our website and why we place such a massive emphasis on DISC and other tools that support, train and develop your team.

You will also learn how to use these skills and observations at home and socially not just at the workplace.

Disc 12 in the Business Essentials Series

Quality Recruitment.

Recruitment of the right people for the right reasons in the right roles for your team is so incredibly important yet so often ignored or pushed to the rear.

You will learn who the right person is for your business and the role you want filled.
You will be able to identify the right people early in the process to save yourself and them the time and money wasted with antique recruitment methodologies that just don't work anymore.

How to get the best out of your recruitment activities so you can keep the assets you acquire for the long term and get the best return from your investment.

ABOUT THE AUTHOR

John Millar is the Managing Director, Senior Business Coach Trainer and Consultant with More Profit Less Time Pty Ltd and CEO-ONDEMAND. Along with his many other business interests, John is proud to have been an associate of the most successful coaching team in the world.

He is recognized as a global leader and has been benchmarked against over 1,300 colleagues in 31 countries. John has over 25 years of hands-on ownership, management, coaching, and entrepreneurial experience in a broad range of industry sectors, including retail, wholesale, import, export, IT, trades and trade services, automotive, primary production, food services, transport, manufacturing, mining, professional services, the fitness industry, and more.

He has extensive experience developing and providing training for small to medium-sized companies and a variety of publicly listed corporate companies. John is an accomplished and talented public and professional speaker. He has been a mentor working with sales/management activities for businesses with a turnover under $100,000 per annum, over $100 million turnover, and everything in between, with great success.

John currently works with business owners and their teams across Australia and has a "Whatever it takes" attitude that has enabled him to help his clients grow their business profits by up to 800%.

 If you are ready to be coached by one of the best in the business, register at:

www.ceo-ondemand.com.au

Make sure to visit www.moreprofitlesstime.com for the new online Management Development Program: The Business Essentials Series.

ACCLAIM FOR JOHN MILLAR'S
Business Coaching and Training in their own words...

"Without John Millar as my Business Coach I wouldn't have a business today."—Grant Jennings Managing Director, Jigsaw Projects

"Taking the decision to be coached and trained by John Millar was carefully considered after experiencing those who over promised and under delivered. I am pleased to say the content of his courses are the tools we all need to master as business owners. His delivery is engaging, thought provoking and empowering and after every session l came away re-energised. John always makes himself available for business building advice both via Skype and face to face beyond the scope of delivery. With his extensive personal experience in building small businesses, he knows and understands what it takes to establish and grow a business. I have no hesitation endorsing John Millar as an educator and business coach and the bonus is he is a very nice person."—Anne Lederman Managing Director FB Salons"

Johns training with my management team was excellent, it was very different from the business coaching and support I have had in the past. John was clear, thoughtful and he addressed the issues we needed to cover without us even knowing they were being addressed! His follow up has been fantastic and exactly what I needed. I would recommend John and his team to anyone looking at getting some business coaching and training done" —Wendy Crawford, Peopleworx

"In my dealings with John as our business coach, I have found him to be a motivated and insightful agent of positive change. He is able to burrow down to the root cause of issues and introduce effective forms of measurement. John then identifies and implements practical solutions and is there to provide the gentle persuasion required to ensure that results are achieved." —Mark Felton, Lindale Insurances

"You have coached and trained us so well throughout the year that we are now used to & find it easy to prepare a 90 day plan, then breaks it down to actionable bite size pieces. Planning in business & personal life certainly is important. It allows us to identify the important things & the bigger picture. Thank you for your support & guidance throughout the year. And not to mention your insight, external perspective to review & assist our business moving forward." —Linda Turner, Director Roy A McDonald Certified Practicing Accountants

"If you want to achieve sales results you never thought were possible and give yourself a competitive edge my strong suggestion is to engage John services and listen closely to what John has to say, during the time I was trained by John I was one of eight sales consultants in a national business for 10 out of the 13 months I lead the sales tally and in 1 quarter I generated three times the revenue of the national sales force combined. Johns training and experience was well worth the investment and paid big dividends. Thanks John." —Julian Fadini, Bellvue Capital

"John is a very enthusiastic trainer and business coach, he is very passionate about getting business owners and their team where they need to be. He goes the extra mile to keep ahead of the latest developments which he then uses to benefit his clients." —Darren Reddy CPA

"I have been to a few seminars and heard John speak numerous times about sales, marketing and business. He is a very knowledgeable and extremely enthusiastic business coach in all his interactions and I would recommend him to all business owners who need a sales and marketing boost!" —Andrew Heath, Managing Director, Fresh Living Group

"I worked with John Millar and found his business knowledge, passion and innovation to be inspiring. He has always been able to set (and achieve) strategic long and short-term goals both for himself and his clients without losing that personal connection he builds with everyone he meets. He has been and I believe will continue to be a strong mentor and trainer for anyone wanting to take that next step in their business." —Bree Webster, Online Marketing Guru

"Massive Action Day" – what an understatement, John Millars 4 hour frenzy challenged me to seriously review areas of my business I would not have gone to …. In this way, the process identified incongruence's in my mind, my business and my modus operandi. It's created a paradigm shift. Thanks John, the road map just got a whole lot clearer. Your friendship and insights since 2003 have been a gift to my business and I." —Andrew Reay, Counsellor, Hypnotherapist and Counsellor, Thinkshift Transformations

"John Millar is not your usual Business coach or trainer; he gets involved with you and your business and provides hands on help to make sure you follow through on his advice. He is highly motivated to help his clients and his personal guarantee certainly shows this. He has now transposed his thoughts, advice and love of good business onto a series of DVD's in his business venture – More Profit Less Time. This has excellent tips and advice for anyone either starting out or already in business. I highly recommend John to any business owner who wants to run a business and not a j.o.b.!" —Darren Cassidy, Managing Director HR2U

"I and many of my Business Partners and colleagues have worked with John since 2010 as our business oath, trainer and motivator and found him to be an extremely motivational person to assist us achieve our business goals. This company and its products allows for John's skill set to be accessed by a wider number of potential clients. His very professional DVD series is extremely good value for money and is easily accessible for all of us who are time poor. If you are looking to maximise your and your business's results and to start achieving your goals and dreams, contact John; you won't look back!!" —Mark Cleland, Mortgage Choice

"John develops real relationships with the people he comes into contact with. He is pasionate about what he does. His DVD and group training series, is full of good ideas and process to make your business better. Knowing what to do and actually doing it are two different things. John is excellent at helping you get things done." —Carey Rudd, Sales Director, Online Knowledge

"I have known John since 2004 and found him to be extremely knowledgably in both Sales and Business systems as a business coach without peer. John has provided me with business advice as well as personal coaching over the years, helping me with the running of my organisation. I'm impressed with John's DVD series where he has condensed a lot of the information in an easy to follow format that any business owner can use immediately. I wish he had released these DVDs earlier, as they are a goldmine of information, and practical how to that allow anyone to increase the profit in their business and get back valuable wasted time." —Steve Psaradellis, Managing Director, TEBA

"John's DVD and workbook delivery of his no-nonsense advice provides a low-cost option for those business owners looking to set and achieve goals that will increase profit. I found the conversational style of the DVD's easy to follow, whilst the requirement to pause the DVD and write down some action points ensured a level of commitment to the advice being provided." — Mark Felton, Lindale Insurances

"I only met John briefly at a BNI meeting and knew instantly i need to hire him for my business as my business coach. His attitude towards work and how to improve my cash line had an instant effect on before, even before I finally hired him on an official basis. I found myself thinking "what would John do" and this was only after just meeting him. I cannot see my business expend and give me "More Profit Less Time" without John's expert direction and training. If you want to succeed in business life, you need John Millar, without him you're just kidding yourself " —Leslie Cachia, Managing Director, Letac Drafting

"I can highly recommend John Millar to any business owner who wants to grow his business. When I hear very positive feedback from colleagues who are skeptics by nature about John's ability and skills, I know John will help all those he comes in contact with. John comes with a selfless nature and the willingness to work inside a client's business to make it succeed. Rare indeed!" —Darren Cassidy, Managing Director, HR2U"I first met John Millar in mid-2010 and have always found him to be of an honest and generous character that engenders an easy association with him. I love how easy he is to listen to and how passionate he is about his work and topics. John demonstrates a love for life and his work and I have no hesitation in recommending his services." —Kathie M Thomas, Managing Director, VA

"I have listened to John speak on a number of occasions and find him a very knowledgeable speaker with a passion for what he does. I have also interacted with a number of his clients and they all tell me that he helps them achieve results in their business. If you are looking for business help John is a person you can trust." —Carey Rudd, Sales Director, Online Knowledge

"John knows his stuff, he knows how the get results, John has so many great ideas in building a business and helping business owners work less and make more money. John has released a DVD set on doing just that. I have watched the 1st one and it was great, very informative and easy to understand, I happily recommend John to anyone in need of help and guidance" —Frank Eramo, Proprietor, Dynotune

"I have known John only for a short time, however the impact that he has had on me, not just my business has helped me to visualise opportunities that I began to doubt my ability to realise. He is encouraging and at the same time challenging so that he can/you can, begin to see how to maximise the business potential, John calls it being an unreasonable friend, I call it being a mate. If you have any questions about the direction of your business, if you want to seem your bottom line improve not just turnover but real profit, if you want a person who will work with you then I strongly recommend that you engage him at your earliest convenience. John is the best thing that has happened to my business. I could tell you about the way he is on track to make 1/2 a million for me on his contacts alone, but that actually sells him short, he has become like my partner in business, and cares about my success as if it was his own, we will flourish because I took the step to employ his training to help me grow. If you get a chance to get him training you, don't wait like I did, get in as quickly as possible, his time is your business and if like me your business is to make money, then every day you don't have him on retainer you lose money." —Russell Summers, Managing Director, The Give Life Centre

"It's usually easy to be mediocre in business but it's impossible when you have John Millar training you. He has been my right hand since 2003!" —David Manser, CFO, Hydrosteer

"I now have a commercial, profitable business and now it's my choice when I work IN my business and when I work ON it and have had john helping me in business since 1988. I can't imagine not having John as a part of our business." —David Wall, Director, D&K Transport

"The work John has done since 2008 coaching and training our marketing team, administration and finance teams, buyers, store managers and staff nationally have been fantastic." —Ross Sudano, Director, Anaconda Adventure Stores

"John is a creative, professional, practical and committed business coach and trainer. His approach since we first met him in 1994 to working with a client team through the application of useful tools, information and anecdotes along with his easy going & easy to understand delivery sets him apart from other business coaches that I have used in the past." —Anthony Beasley, Director, The Astra Group

"I have worked with John Millar for the since 2004 and I didn't think it was possible to achieve what we have achieved together. His business coaching, training and services just get better and better!" —Terrance Chong, Managing Director, Echo Graphics and Printing

"John's business coaching, training and support has transformed our business across Australia and New Zealand since 2008."—Rose Vis, Managing Director, VIP Australia

"We first met John in 2005, he is AMAZING at sales, marketing, operations, logistics, finance training and so much more. Since engaging John as our business coach our business has exploded, our team are happy, our clients are raving about us and my husband and I now take at least 12 weeks holidays a year, EVERY year." —Shirley Du, Director, Goldline Technology

"It's the no nonsense results driven business coaching and training focus John bought to the table that had such a massive effect on our business." —David Runkel, Director, Tracomp Fabrication and Steel

"We started working with John in early 2010, within 90 days of working with and being trained by John Millar we had the biggest and most profitable month in our 15 year history. That's impressive." —Hugh Gilchrist, Managing Director, Australian Moulding Company

"If you don't have John as your business trainer you aren't meeting your business potential." —Don Robertson, Director, Medallion Electrical Services

Thank You